MARGARET MORGAN
and
MARY MORGAN PEDLOW

Memorial

RIVERSIDE PUBLIC LIBRARY

INSIDE THE NFL

NFC SOUTH

BY JIM LOGAN

LIBRARY OF CONGRESS CATALOGING-IN-PUBLICATION DATA

Logan, Jim, 1958-
  NFC South / by Jim Logan.
    p. cm. — (Inside the NFL)
  Includes bibliographical references and index.
  ISBN 1-59296-514-8 (library bound : alk. paper) 1. National Football League—
History—Juvenile literature. 2. Football—United States—History—Juvenile literature.
I. Title: National Football Conference South. II. Title. III. Series.
  GV955.5.N35L64 2006
  796.332'64'0973—dc22   2005004803

Children's Room

ACKNOWLEDGEMENTS

The Child's World®: Mary Berendes, Publishing Director

Editorial Directions, Inc.: Russell Primm, Editorial Director and Line Editor; Matt
Messbarger, Project Editor; Elizabeth K. Martin, Assistant Editor; Olivia Nellums,
Editorial Assistant; Susan Hindman, Copy Editor; Susan Ashley, Beth Franken,
Proofreaders; Kevin Cunningham, Fact Checker; Tim Griffin/IndexServ, Indexer;
James Buckley Jr., Photo Researcher and Selector

The Design Lab: Kathleen Petelinsek, Design and Page Production

Photos: Cover: David Bergman/Corbis
AP: 7, 25; Brian Bahr/Getty: 21; Al Bello/Getty: 38; Chuck Burton/AP: 16;
Stephen J. Carrera/AP: 28; Pete Cosgrove/AP: 39; Scott Cunningham/Getty:
2; Ric Feld/AP: 12; Focus on Sport/Getty: 26; Chris Graythen/Getty: 1, 31, 32;
Jed Jacobsohn/Getty: 42; Craig Jones/Getty: 22; M. David Leeds/Getty: 11;
Andy Lyons/Getty: 10; Steve Nesius/AP: 14; Doug Pensinger/Getty: 41; Sports
Gallery/Al Messerschmidt: 9, 19, 20, 30, 34, 35, 37

TABLE OF CONTENTS

Published in the United States of America by
The Child's World® • PO Box 326
Chanhassen, MN 55317-0326
800-599-READ • www.childsworld.com

The Child's World

INTRODUCTION

ATLANTA FALCONS

Year Founded: 1966

Home Stadium: Georgia Dome

Year Stadium Opened: 1992

Team Colors: Black and red

CAROLINA PANTHERS

Year Founded: 1995

Home Stadium: Ericsson Stadium

Year Stadium Opened: 1996

Team Colors: Black, blue, and silver

If you think of the National Football League (NFL) as a family, the teams of the National Football Conference (NFC) South are the younger brothers who are showing that they're ready to play with the big boys. It's also a division where the fans have needed a lot of patience. For years, it was the NFL's only division in which none of its teams had won a championship. And then came the Tampa Bay Buccaneers in 2002. The team that lost its first 26 games destroyed the Oakland Raiders in Super Bowl XXXVII. Suddenly, football's little brother was the man of the house.

It wasn't easy getting there. You might say the NFC South, which was created when the league changed the way its teams are organized in 2002, has endured its share of growing pains. This is a fairly young division of expansion teams. The oldest franchise began play in 1966, while the youngest first fielded a team in 1995. The three oldest—the Atlanta Falcons, New Orleans Saints and Buccaneers—all suffered for a long time. Wins were rare and success seemed a long way off. At the end of the 2002 season those three teams had a combined record of 634–961–11. That's a lot of lean years.

But that was the past. Today, the NFC South looks like a contender for years to come.

The Falcons feature one of pro football's emerging superstars in electrifying quarterback Michael Vick and a stalwart defense that contributed greatly to the club's rise to the top of the division standings in 2004. The Buccaneers won a Super Bowl in the 2002 season with a dominating defense and great players in their prime. The Saints are showing signs of being very good. And the Carolina Panthers took the league by storm with an exciting and surprising run to the Super Bowl in the 2003 season.

All four clubs also are led by some of the most innovative young coaches in the game today: Atlanta's Jim Mora Jr., Carolina's John Fox, New Orleans' Jim Haslett, and Tampa Bay's Jon Gruden. Gruden, in fact, was only 39 years old when the Buccaneers won Super Bowl XXXVII in the 2002 season. He is the youngest coach ever to lead his team to a Super Bowl win.

This is a division that is seeing the rise of its first true superstars, players who will help their teams be dangerous for years. Let's take a look at these four unique teams.

NEW ORLEANS SAINTS

Year Founded: 1967

Home Stadium: Louisiana Superdome

Year Stadium Opened: 1975

Team Colors: Black and gold

TAMPA BAY BUCCANEERS

Year Founded: 1976

Home Stadium: Raymond James Stadium

Year Stadium Opened: 1998

Team Colors: Red, pewter, and black

CHAPTER ONE

THE ATLANTA FALCONS

The oldest team in the NFC South was also the first one to make it to a Super Bowl. The Falcons won the NFC title in 1998 and played in Super Bowl XXXIII. It was a long and rocky road getting there from the team's beginnings in 1966.

The Falcon's first **draft** choice was their first victory. They took linebacker Tommy Nobis of the University of Texas with the first overall pick in the 1966 draft. Nobis had also been picked by the Houston Oilers, of the rival **American Football League** (AFL). American astronauts orbiting Earth begged Nobis to sign with Houston, home of the space program. However, Nobis went with Atlanta and gave the Falcons 11 great years. Norb Hecker, the team's first coach, didn't last as long. The Falcons posted a 3–11 record their first year, 1966, and went 1–12–1 the next. After losing their first three games of 1968, Hecker was replaced by Norm Van Brocklin. The Falcons finished with a 2–12 record.

Finally, in 1971, the team earned its first

Atlanta originally was awarded an AFL franchise in June 1965. Three weeks later, the city was awarded an NFL team, and the AFL deal fell through.

Linebacker Tommy Nobis (No. 60) was the Falcons' first star.

winning record, 7–6–1. Two years later, the Falcons went 9–5, but the 1970s mostly were a tough time for the team. Some good, though, came out of that decade. In 1975, they drafted quarterback Steve Bartkowski of the University of California-Berkeley with the first pick overall in the draft.

The Falcons' NFC West championship in 1980 ended the rival Rams' seven-year stranglehold on the division crown.

With Bartkowski running the offense and the defense pounding opponents, the Falcons went 9–7 in 1978. They beat the Philadelphia Eagles in the first round of the playoffs but lost to the Dallas Cowboys in the next round.

Bartkowski's best year was 1980, when the Falcons won the NFC West (their old division) with a 12–4 record. They were nearly unstoppable. Bartkowski threw for 31 touchdown passes, the best in the league, and running backs William Andrews and Lynn Cain combined for nearly 2,000 yards rushing.

Once again, though, the Cowboys ended their season. This time it really hurt. The Falcons were ahead, 24–10, going into the fourth quarter. Then Dallas quarterback Danny White led his team to three touchdowns, the last one a 23-yard pass with 42 seconds left in the game. Final score: Cowboys 30, Falcons 27.

In the next 10 years, the Falcons had just one winning season—1982—and that season had only nine games because of a players' strike. A bright spot was Billy "White Shoes" Johnson, a dazzling kick returner and receiver. Big Gerald Riggs was a human battering ram at running back. It wasn't until 1990, when Jerry Glanville was hired as coach, that the team had better luck.

In 1991, with Deion "Prime Time" Sanders anchoring the defensive backfield, the Falcons swaggered to a 10–6 record. They looked ready to make a run through the playoffs after beating New Orleans in the first round. However, they lost to Washington in their next game. After back-to-back 6–10 seasons, Glanville was gone.

Steve Bartkowski is Atlanta's all-time leading passer.

June Jones, a former Falcons backup quarterback, was hired as coach in 1994. The same year, the team acquired rocket-armed quarterback Jeff George in a trade from the Indianapolis Colts.

The Falcons posted a 7–9 record in George's first season. The

Craig Heyward's punishing running earned him the nickname "Ironhead."

next year, they went 9–7 behind Craig "Ironhead" Heyward's 1,083 rushing yards. They lost to the Green Bay Packers, 37–20, in the first round of the playoffs.

The 1996 season was disappointing. Atlanta staggered to 3–13, and soon Jones was replaced by Dan Reeves.

The Falcons shocked the NFL in 1998 by posting a franchise-best record of 14–2 and earning a

Dan Reeves took over as coach in 1997 and guided Atlanta to its first Super Bowl the next season.

Quarterback Michael Vick thrills fans with his acrobatic style.

trip to Super Bowl XXXIII against the Denver Broncos. Veteran quarterback Chris Chandler and star running back Jamal Anderson led Atlanta. But if the Falcons were the Cinderella team, the Broncos and quarterback John Elway were the clock striking midnight. Elway passed for 336 yards, and Denver's Terrell Davis ran for 102 more. Meanwhile, the Broncos' defense kept Chandler and Anderson from doing much damage. Final score: Broncos 34, Falcons 19.

As they had since they started, the Falcons followed their good season with disappointing years, posting losing records in their next three seasons.

And then the future arrived in the person of an athletic lefty named Michael Vick. The Falcons took the quarterback from Virginia Tech with the first pick overall in the 2001 draft. Blessed with a cannon for an arm and speed that one player called "pretty close to cheetah," Vick is proving to be what other players admiringly call a freak.

"You have to understand this guy is changing the game," Vikings linebacker Henry Crockett said. "He's got the same skills that John Elway had, just five-tenths of a second faster." Or as Buccaneers linebacker Simeon Rice said, "I couldn't put a limit on him at all. He's taking his offense to another dimension."

In Vick's first full season as a starter in 2002, the Falcons won nine games and earned a wild-card playoff berth. But if those wins weren't enough to convince Atlanta fans of his importance to the team, they learned the hard way the next year. Vick broke his leg in the preseason and missed most of the year, and the Falcons won only five games. That cost Reeves his job.

Jim Mora Jr. was hired as coach and reenergized a defense led by end Patrick Kerney, who earned a **Pro Bowl** berth after making 13 sacks (tackling

Patrick Kerney (No. 97) and the Falcons' defense helped carry the team to the conference championship game in 2004.

Michael Vick set an NFL record for quarterbacks by rushing for 173 yards in a victory over Minnesota in 2002.

a quarterback behind the line of scrimmage). A healthy Vick took charge of the offense again, and Atlanta won 11 regular-season games and the NFC South championship.

Atlanta fans hope the next step is a Super Bowl victory.

CHAPTER TWO

THE CAROLINA PANTHERS

Somebody forgot to tell the Carolina Panthers that expansion teams don't win much in their first season, because they did just that. In their first year, 1995, they had a 7–9 record. That was four more wins than any other first-year expansion club.

The wins came on the field, but they started with the hard work done by the team's owners and management long before any player put on his uniform.

When the NFL made Carolina the league's 29th franchise in 1993, owner Jerry Richardson got to work. Richardson was a former wide receiver for the Colts who had become a successful restaurant company owner. He hired experienced football men to run the club, and they made smart moves. First, they hired Dom Capers, who had been the Pittsburgh Steelers's defensive coordinator, as head coach. Then they picked a team.

Earlier expansion teams usually got players other clubs didn't want. The Panthers avoided that by signing veteran **free agents.**

> The Panthers are based in Charlotte, North Carolina. However, they played their first season at Clemson University in South Carolina—a two-hour drive from Charlotte.

Kevin Greene and the Panthers took the NFL by surprise in 1996.

Linebackers Carlton Bailey, Lamar Lathon, and Sam Mills were signed that way. Receiver Willie Green and running back Derrick Moore also helped the team right away.

Carolina used its three first-round draft picks wisely. Quarterback Kerry Collins, tackle Blake Brockermeyer, and cornerback Tyrone Poole all started and played well.

The mix of veterans and rookies worked like magic. At one point, the Panthers won four games in a row, including a defeat of the mighty San Francisco 49ers.

What the Panthers did in their second year was simply amazing. Linebacker Kevin Greene led the league with 14.5 sacks. He led a defense that was second in the NFL in fewest points allowed—only 218 in 16 games! On offense, Collins showed signs

of greatness. Running back Anthony Johnson ran for 1,120 yards. Kicker John Kasay had a league-high 37 field goals. Put the numbers together and they added up to a 12–4 record.

In the first round of the playoffs, the Panthers beat the defending Super Bowl champion Cowboys, 26–17. The defense helped do its part by knocking out Dallas wide receiver Michael Irvin early in the game. With his number-one target out, Cowboys quarterback Troy Aikman struggled and threw three **interceptions.**

Brett Favre and the Packers ended the Panthers' season in the NFC Championship Game, 30–13. Carolina's **blitzing** was ineffective, and the Packers rushed for a surprisingly easy 201 yards. Still, seven Carolina players were named to the NFC Pro Bowl team, Capers was coach of the year, and it looked like the Panthers would be a power-house team for years to come.

Then came the 1997 season. Collins broke his jaw in a preseason game against the Denver Broncos and had a tough year, throwing 21 interceptions with just 11 touchdowns. The Panthers wobbled to a 7–9 record.

The next year was worse. Four games into the season, Collins was **released** by the team. Steve Beuerlein stepped in as quarterback, but the Panthers never got in gear and finished 4–12. Capers was fired and replaced by George Seifert. Seifert had a record of success. He had won two Super Bowls and 108 games in his eight years as coach of the 49ers.

In Seifert's first year, 1999, the Panthers were better, but they still finished 8–8. The highlight of

When the Panthers knocked off the 49ers in 1995, it was the first time in NFL history that a first-year expansion team had beaten a defending Super Bowl champion.

the season was the passing game. Beuerlein threw for 4,436 yards and 36 touchdowns, most of them to wide receivers Muhsin Muhammad and Patrick Jeffers and tight end Wesley Walls.

After a 7–9 season in 2000, the Panthers fell

Steve Beuerlein passed for a whopping 4,436 yards in 1999.

Muhsin Muhammad is the Panthers' all-time leading receiver.

apart in 2001. With 2000 **Heisman Trophy** winner Chris Weinke at quarterback, Carolina won just one game. It wasn't all Weinke's fault. Although the offense was the second worst in the league, the defense ranked dead last. Seifert was let go.

For 2002, John Fox, defensive coordinator for the New York

John Fox's fiery coaching took Carolina to its first Super Bowl in the 2003 season.

Quarterback Jake Delhomme has become an elite quarterback.

THE CAROLINA PANTHERS

Giants the previous five seasons, was hired as coach. With a roster of young players sprinkled with veterans, Fox's initial team showed immediate, and dramatic, improvement. The Panthers won their first three games under their fiery new leader and went 7–9 in 2002.

The promise of that season was fulfilled the next year. Jake Delhomme, a free-agent signee from New Orleans, took over as quarterback and passed for 3,219 yards and Fox's defense, featuring young defensive end Julius Peppers, was one of the best in the league. Carolina won 11 games and cruised to the NFC South championship.

After beating Dallas 29–10 in the opening round of the playoffs, the visiting Panthers stunned St. Louis in the divisional round, winning 29–23 on Delhomme's 69-yard touchdown strike to Steve Smith on the first play of the second overtime. For the second time in its brief history, Carolina was in the NFC title game. And this time, the Panthers won it. They reached their first Super Bowl by upsetting host Philadelphia 14–3.

Though Super Bowl XXXVIII resulted in an agonizing, 32–29 loss to New England, the 2003 season was an unqualified success. The next year wasn't as kind to Carolina: key injuries, such as those to Smith and running back Stephen Davis, contributed to a disastrous 1–7 start. But six wins in the next seven games left Panthers fans anxious for the start of a new year.

CHAPTER THREE

THE NEW ORLEANS SAINTS

If there's a moral in the New Orleans Saints' story, it's that patience pays—even if you have to wait 20 years. Amazingly, that's how long the Saints had to wait before they enjoyed their first winning season.

When the Saints entered the NFL in 1967, the **expansion draft** was a tough way to build a team. The players available were not wanted by their old teams, and few were good enough to build a team around. The Saints found this out when they selected two former Green Bay Packers running backs: future Hall of Famer Paul Hornung and onetime great Jim Taylor.

Unfortunately for the Saints, Hornung retired before training camp and Taylor played just one season, then retired as well.

One player who did help the team was quarterback Billy Kilmer, who put up good numbers even if the Saints didn't win much. Kilmer eventually was traded to the Washington Redskins, but not before he got to see one of the greatest plays in Saints

New Orleans was awarded an NFL franchise on November 1, 1966—All Saints' Day.

Tom Dempsey made this kick from an NFL-record 63 yards.

history. In 1970, Tom Dempsey kicked an NFL-record
63-yard field goal on the final play against the
Detroit Lions.

Dempsey was born with half a right foot and no
right hand. He kicked with a special boot. With just
two seconds to play and the Saints on their own 45-
yard line, coach J. D. Roberts looked over at Dempsey

Archie Manning is the Saints' all-time leading passer.

and said, "Give it your best shot." His stunning kick gave the Saints a 19–17 victory.

Such great moments were few and far between, though. Not even great players like quarterback Archie Manning, the second player taken in the 1971 draft, could help. Although Manning was a wizard with the football, he was usually the best player on the field. Through the years, the Saints drafted some good players—including running backs Chuck Muncie and George Rogers and wide receiver Wes Chandler—but not enough of them.

The club went through a string of coaches with no better luck. Not even a new stadium, the Louisiana Superdome, helped. The Saints made it their home in 1975 and won only two games that year.

What is surely the team's low point came in 1980. New Orleans was coming off an 8–8 season and hopes were high. But the Saints stumbled to a 1–15 season. Fans started coming to games with paper bags over their heads and calling the team "the Aints."

The team's luck began to change in 1985. New owner Tom Benson hired respected football man Jim Finks as general manager. Finks hired Jim Mora, who had been a winner in the United States Football League (USFL), as head coach. In his first season, 1986, the Saints finished at 7–9. Running back Rueben Mayes gained 1,353 yards and was named Rookie of the Year.

Finally, in 1987, the Saints were winners. Twenty years after the birth of the franchise, New Orleans posted an amazing 12–3 record.

The Saints made running back Ricky Williams their entire draft in 1999.

The fans loved quarterback Bobby Hebert, a Louisiana native from Baton Rouge. The season ended with a 44–10 loss to the Vikings in the playoffs.

Under Mora, the Saints were competitive and reached the playoffs in 1990, 1991, and 1992. The high point came in 1992, when the defense led the NFL in fewest points allowed (202) and in sacks (57) to finish with a 12–4 record. The Saints lost in the first round of playoffs to the Philadelphia Eagles.

The Mora era ended in 1996. Mike Ditka, who had led the Chicago Bears to victory in Super Bowl XX, eventually was hired as head coach. After consecutive 6–10 seasons, Ditka shocked the football world. He announced that he would trade all the Saints' draft picks for the fifth overall pick. With it, he chose Heisman Trophy winner Ricky Williams of Texas. Unfortunately, Williams struggled to adjust to the NFL and the Saints finished 3–13 in 1999. Ditka was fired.

In 2000, former Saints assistant coach and defensive coordinator Jim Haslett was hired as head coach and made an immediate impact. He led the team to its second division title and, 33 years after it was founded, its first playoff victory. New Orleans won a 31–28 nail-biter over the defending Super Bowl champion St. Louis Rams. Although the Saints lost to the Vikings in the next round, the message was clear: The New Orleans Saints were winners.

Aaron Brooks passed for more than 3,500 yards each year from 2001 to 2004.

Tom Dempsey's record 63-yard field goal in 1970 came in J. D. Roberts' first game as the Saints' head coach.

With a tough, stingy defense and young offensive standouts like running back Deuce McAllister and receiver Donte' Stallworth, the Saints appeared primed for a march into the Super Bowl.

It hasn't worked out that way—yet. Though New Orleans has won at least eight games each year since

2002, the Saints have found themselves on the outside looking in at playoff time.

In 2004, for instance, Brooks passed for 3,810 yards, McAllister rushed for 1,074 yards, and wide receiver Joe Horn tied his own club record with 94 catches. On the last weekend of the season, the Saints knocked division-rival Carolina

Running back Deuce McAllister threatens to score every time he touches the ball.

Sure-handed Joe Horn is one of the NFL's top wide receivers.

out of playoff contention with a 21–18 victory. But they needed help to reach the postseason themselves and didn't get it, missing out instead on a tiebreaker.

So it was wait until next year again for New Orleans. But the one thing Saints' fans have learned is that good things do come to those who wait!

CHAPTER FOUR

THE TAMPA BAY BUCCANEERS

Of the four teams in the NFC South, none had a more humbling start than the Buccaneers. They lost every game of their first season in 1976 and the first 12 of 1977. That's 26 games. And yet, 26 years after they first took the field, they won Super Bowl XXXVII. How they got there is a story of patience and perseverance.

Tampa Bay became the NFL's 27th franchise in 1974. When the Buccaneers stepped on the field for the first time two years later they were coached by John McKay, who had won four national championships at the University of Southern California (USC). McKay had a plan for making the Bucs title contenders, and he stuck with it even in the team's darkest hours.

That first team, which played in the AFC West before moving to the NFC Central the next season, had one true star: defensive end Lee Roy Selmon. The Bucs made Selmon their No. 1 draft pick, and he went on to earn a place in the Pro Football Hall of Fame. But first, he and the rest of the Bucs had to survive that first grueling season.

> **The team changed colors and logos in 1997, the same year they had their first winning season since 1982.**

Tailback Ricky Bell ran for coach John McKay in college at USC and in the pros at Tampa Bay.

It wasn't easy. The offense scored more than 20 points only once, and the defense had trouble stopping anybody. McKay, when asked what he thought of the team's execution, replied, "I'm in favor of it."

The losing streak finally ended in 1977 when the Bucs' defense came up with three interceptions for

Lee Roy Selmon was a Hall of Fame defensive end.

Ricky Bell gained 1,263 yards for the 1979 division champs.

touchdowns in a 33–14 victory over the Saints.

The Bucs were the talk of the NFL when they won their first five games in 1979. Led by quarterback Doug Williams and former USC tailback Ricky Bell, Tampa Bay made it to the NFC title game against the Los Angeles Rams. The offense, however, couldn't get going and the Rams won, 9–0.

Linebacker Larry Ball is the only man who played for Miami's undefeated 1972 team and Tampa Bay's win-less 1976 team.

The Bucs made the playoffs in 1981 and 1982, then the dark times returned. After two more frustrating years, McKay retired after the 1984 season. In the 13 seasons from 1983 to 1995, the Bucs averaged 11 losses and won more than six games just once.

In 1995, the team got new ownership and, it seems, a fresh start. Tony Dungy was brought in to lead the Bucs in 1996. They started slow, but finished strong to post a 6–10 record.

The next year Tampa Bay used a ferocious defense and solid running game to record its first winning record, 10–6, in 16 years. The defense revolved around tackle Warren Sapp, who was as talkative as he was dominating. The offense was powered by the running team of Warrick Dunn and Mike Alstott. Dunn, the league's offensive Rookie of the Year, darted and slashed his way to 978 yards rushing. Alstott was a bulldozer in shoulder pads who piled up 665 yards.

The high point of the Dungy era came in 1999, when the Bucs posted a franchise-best 11–5 record and advanced it to the NFC Championship Game against the Rams. In a brutal defensive struggle, the Bucs fell short, 11–6. Sapp was named the league's defensive player of the year.

After the 2001 season, Dungy was replaced by the fiery Jon Gruden. The Bucs paid a steep price to pry Gruden away from the Oakland Raiders. They gave Oakland $8 million and four high draft choices. Gruden showed he was worth it.

In the 2002 regular season, Tampa Bay posted a 12–4 record

Mike Alstott can run around opponents or through them.

Safety Dexter Jackson was the Most Valuable Player (MVP) of Super Bowl XXXVII.

and roared through the playoffs to earn their first trip to the Super Bowl. Their opponent: Gruden's old team, the Raiders.

It looked like a classic matchup. The Raiders, behind the passing of league MVP Rich Gannon, had the NFL's No. 1 offense. The Bucs boasted the No. 1 defense. Something had to give.

It was the Raiders.

The Bucs' defense made Gannon look like a rookie. They intercepted him five times. They set a record by running three picks back for touchdowns. Safety Dexter Jackson picked off two and was named the game's MVP. Gannon also was sacked five times and the Raiders managed just 62 yards in total offense in the first half. On offense, Bucs quarter-

Head coach Jon Gruden (with trophy) and owner Malcolm Glazer enjoyed a victory ride after Super Bowl XXXVII.

back Brad Johnson completed 18 of 34 passes for 215 yards and two touchdowns. Receiver Keenan McCardell caught two touchdown passes. Running back Michael Pittman rushed for 124 yards. Five minutes into the third quarter the Bucs led, 34–3.

The Raiders tried to make a game of it, but the Bucs' defense was just too much. Sapp and defensive lineman Simeon Rice wreaked havoc in the middle. Linebackers Derrick Brooks and Shelton Quarles stuffed both run and pass. Cornerback Dwight Smith returned two interceptions for touchdowns. Cornerback Brian Kelly had a team-high eight tackles and smothered Raiders receivers Tim Brown and Jerry Rice.

Final score: 48–21. For the Bucs, it was heaven. For the rest of the NFL, it meant trouble.

"We're young, we're good, we're going to have to be [reckoned] with a long time," said Smith.

It sure seemed that way at the time. But the ensuing years have not followed the plan. Tampa Bay dropped off to seven wins the season after its Super Bowl victory, then, shockingly, to only five wins in 2004.

The Buccaneers set a Super Bowl record by returning three interceptions for touchdowns in their 48–21 rout of Oakland in game XXXVII.

Though the defense remains a force, with Brooks and cornerback Ronde Barber leading the way, the offense has not kept up. There are glimmers of hope, though. Brian Griese, the son of Pro Football Hall of Famer Bob Griese, became the quarterback in 2004 and passed for 2,632 yards and 20 touchdowns. His favorite target was rookie wide receiver Michael Clayton, who caught 80 passes for 1,193 yards.

Pro Bowl cornerback Ronde Barber (with ball) and the Buccaneers' defense remain a formidable force.

STAT STUFF

T E A M   R E C O R D S

TEAM	ALL-TIME RECORD	NFL TITLES (MOST RECENT)	NUMBER OF TIMES IN PLAYOFFS	TOP COACH (WINS)
Atlanta	237–349–6	1 (2002)	8	Don Reeves (52)
Carolina	71–89–0	0	2	Dom Capers (31)
New Orleans	234–339–5	0	5	Jim Mora (93)
Tampa Bay	172–279–1	0	8	Tony Dungy (56)

Tight end Alge Crumpler and the Falcons ruled the NFC South in 2004.

MORE STAT STUFF

M E M B E R S   O F   T H E   P R O   F O O T B A L L   H A L L   O F   F A M E

ATLANTA		
PLAYER	POSITION	DATE INDUCTED
Eric Dickerson	Running Back	1999
Tommy McDonald	Wide Receiver	1998

CAROLINA		
PLAYER	POSITION	DATE INDUCTED
None		

NEW ORLEANS		
PLAYER	POSITION	DATE INDUCTED
Doug Atkins	Defensive End	1982
Earl Campbell	Running Back	1991
Jim Finks	General Manager	1995
Hank Stram	Coach	2003
Jim Taylor	Fullback	1976

TAMPA BAY		
PLAYER	POSITION	DATE INDUCTED
Lee Roy Selmon	Linebacker	1995
Steve Young	Quarterback	2005

MORE STAT STUFF

N F C   S O U T H   C A R E E R   L E A D E R S   (T H R O U G H   2 0 0 4)

ATLANTA

CATEGORY	NAME (YEARS WITH TEAM)	TOTAL
Rushing yards	Gerald Riggs (1982-88)	6,631
Passing yards	Steve Bartkowski (1975-1985)	23,468
Touchdown passes	Steve Bartkowski (1975-1985)	154
Receptions	Terance Mathis (1994-2001)	573
Touchdowns	Terance Mathis (1994-2001)	57
Scoring	Morten Andersen (1995-2000)	620

CAROLINA

CATEGORY	NAME (YEARS WITH TEAM)	TOTAL
Rushing yards	Tshimanga Biakabutuka (1996-2001)	2,530
Passing yards	Steve Beuerlein (1996-2000)	12,690
Touchdown passes	Steve Beuerlein (1996-2000)	86
Receptions	Muhsin Muhammad (1996-2004)	578
Touchdowns	Wesley Walls (1996-2002)	44
Scoring	John Kasay (1996-2004)	843

NEW ORLEANS

CATEGORY	NAME (YEARS WITH TEAM)	TOTAL
Rushing yards	George Rogers (1981-84)	4,267
Passing yards	Archie Manning (1971-1982)	21,734
Touchdown passes	Archie Manning (1971-1982)	115
Receptions	Eric Martin (1985-1993)	532
Touchdowns	Dalton Hilliard (1986-1993)	53
Scoring	Morten Andersen (1982-1994)	1,318

TAMPA BAY

CATEGORY	NAME (YEARS WITH TEAM)	TOTAL
Rushing yards	James Wilder (1981-89)	5,957
Passing yards	Vinny Testaverde (1987-1992)	14,820
Touchdown passes	Vinny Testaverde (1987-1992)	77
Receptions	James Wilder (1981-89)	430
Touchdowns	Mike Alstott (1996-2004)	61
Scoring	Martin Gramatica (1999-2004)	592

GLOSSARY

American Football League—began play in 1960 as a rival to the NFL

blitzing—rushing the quarterback by the linebackers or defensive backs

draft—held each April, this is when NFL teams choose college players to join their teams; teams with the worst records the prior year choose first, but draft picks can be traded to move a team's draft order

expansion draft—when new teams select players from existing franchises, which make a certain number of players available

free agent—players who sign with any team they can contract with

general manager—the executive who runs the team for the owner; his biggest job is getting the players for the club

Heisman Trophy—the annual award given to the best college football player

interceptions—passes caught by defensive players

Pro Bowl—the NFL's all-star game played in Hawaii after the Super Bowl

released—when a player is let go by his team; it's like being fired from a job

United States Football League—a rival league formed in 1982

TIME LINE

1966 Atlanta Falcons join the NFL

1967 New Orleans Saints begin first season

1971 Falcons post first winning record, 7–6–1

1976 Tampa Bay Buccaneers begin play in the AFC West

1979 Bucs reach NFC Championship Game, lose to Los Angeles Rams

1987 Saints have first winning season, 12–3

1995 Carolina Panthers begin first season

1996 Panthers reach NFC championship game, lose to Green Bay Packers

1998 Falcons reach Super Bowl XXXIII, lose to Denver Broncos

1999 Bucs reach NFC Championship Game, lose to St. Louis Rams

2002 Tampa Bay wins Super Bowl XXXVII

FOR MORE INFORMATION ABOUT

THE NFC SOUTH AND THE NFL

BOOKS

Bell, Lonnie. *The History of the New Orleans Saints.* Mankato, Minn.: Creative Education, 2005.

Buckley, James Jr., and Jerry Rice. *America's Greatest Game.* New York: Hyperion Books for Children, 1998.

Goodman, Michael E. *The History of the Atlanta Falcons.* Mankato, Minn.: Creative Education, 2005.

Goodman, Michael E. *The History of the Carolina Panthers.* Mankato, Minn.: Creative Education, 2005.

Goodman, Michael E. *The History of the Tampa Bay Buccaneers.* Mankato, Minn.: Creative Education, 2005.

MacNow, Glen. *Sports Great Deion Sanders.* Springfield, N.J.: Enslow Publishers, 1999.

Marini, Matt. *Football Top 10.* New York: DK Publishing, 2002.

Nyad, Diana. *Boss of Me: The Keyshawn Johnson Story.* Columbus, Miss.: Kid Genesis, 1999.

Owens, Tom. *Football Stadiums.* Brookfield, Conn.: Millbrook Press, 2001.

Polzer, Tim. *Play Football.* New York: DK Publishing, 2002.

ON THE WEB

Visit our home page for lots of links about the NFC South:

http://www.childsworld.com/links

Note to Parents, Teachers, and Librarians: We routinely verify our Web links to make sure they are safe, active sites—so encourage your readers to check them out!

INDEX

A B O U T   T H E   A U T H O R

Jim Logan is a veteran newspaper writer and editor in Santa Barbara, California. He has covered every major sport at the high school and college level, including football. A lifelong fan of football, his playing career unfortunately peaked and ended in eighth grade!